SEASHELLS

A TRUE BOOK

by

Ann O. Squire

Children's Press®
A Division of Scholastic Inc.

New York Toronto London Auckland Sydney
Mexico City New Delhi Hong Kong
Danbury, Connecticut

Shells that washed ashore

Reading and Content Consultant
Jan Jenner

Author's Dedication
To Emma, Evan, and Bunny

The photograph on the cover shows a collection of different shells. The photograph on the title page shows a banded tulip shell.

Library of Congress Cataloging-in-Publication Data

Squire, Ann.
    Seashells / by Ann O. Squire.
        p.   cm. – (True Books)
    Includes index.
    Summary: An introduction to seashells, discussing the different types
of shells, where they are found, and how they are made.
    ISBN 0-516-22341-0 (lib. bdg.)   0-516-26986-0 (pbk.)
    1. Shells—Juvenile literature. [1. Shells]   I. Title.
QL405.2 S68 2002
594.147'7—dc21   2001005755

Contents

Many different kinds
of seashells wash up
on shore each day.

What Is a Seashell?

What a silly question! Everyone knows what a seashell is. Most people, maybe even you, have walked along a beach and looked for beautiful and interesting shells to take home. But did you know that inside every shell on the beach there once lived a small, soft-bodied

A hard shell protects the soft-bodied oyster that lives inside.

animal called a mollusk? A mollusk needs a shell for the same reason that you need bones: to support and protect the soft parts of its body. But while people have their bones on the inside, a mollusk's shell is on the outside.

About half of the world's mollusks live in the oceans. When a mollusk dies, all that is left behind is an empty shell. Many of these shells eventually wash up on the

These boys are collecting seashells on a beach in Virginia.

beach, where they are picked up by shell collectors.

Seashells are found all over the world, but no single kind of shell is found in every ocean.

Shells from areas with warm water are usually more colorful than shells from oceans with cold water. This is because sunlight and heat can affect the color of the shell.

These bright-colored coquina shells were found in the warm waters off the Florida coast.

Univalves and Bivalves

At first glance, all the shells on the beach may look a lot alike. But if you look carefully, you'll see some differences. Some of the shells are made of two pieces that are joined together by a hinge. Clams, oysters, and scallops are some of the mollusks with

Some shells, such as scallops, are really two pieces that are joined together by a hinge.

hinged shells. Other shells are just one piece, and most of these are twisted or coiled in some way, like snail shells.

This snail is a univalve and lives in a twisted shell.

Mollusks that live inside one shell are called univalves (uni means "one," and valve is the word scientists use instead of "shell"). Those that

A razor clam is just one type of mollusk with a hinged shell.

have two shells joined by a hinge are called bivalves (bi means "two"). Although they are both types of mollusks, univalves and bivalves are very different animals.

Univalves are also called gastropods. This group includes land and marine snails. Like snails that live on land, the marine snail has a head with tentacles that help it feel its way around, eyes on the end of stalks, and a long, raspy "tongue," called a radula. This tongue helps the marine snail saw and tear food. And like land snails and slugs, the marine snail creeps along on a single, large foot. When it is disturbed

A snail uses its tentacles to feel its way from place to place.

or threatened, the marine snail goes into hiding, pulling its entire body inside its shell.

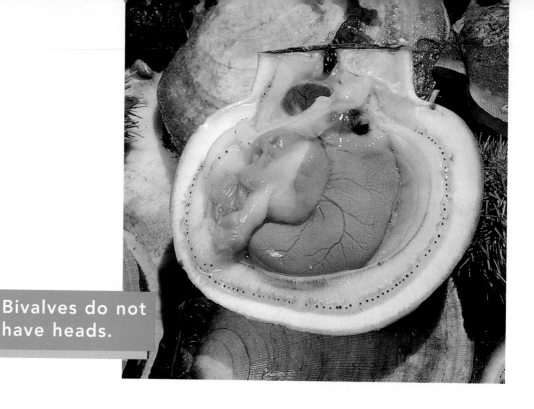

Bivalves do not have heads.

Bivalves, such as clams and oysters, seem much less "animal-like" than their univalve relatives. For one thing, the bivalve doesn't have a head. And while it has a foot, the typical bivalve doesn't move around very much. Instead,

most bivalves anchor them-
selves to rocks, pilings, or the
sea bottom. Some burrow
down into the sand. When a
bivalve is disturbed, it snaps
its two shells together and
holds them tightly closed with
powerful muscles.

Clams usually do not move around
on the floor of the ocean.

Chiton shells are divided into eight plates.

Most of the shells on any beach come from either univalves or bivalves. But you may also find a shell that once housed a different type of mollusk. Chitons are primitive mollusks whose shells are divided into eight plates, somewhat like a coat of armor.

Tusk shells are mollusks that live in shells shaped like an elephant's tusk. And the chambered nautilus, a relative of the octopus, lives inside a spiral shell that it fills with gas to help it float.

The chambered nautilus lives inside a spiral shell.

How Do Shells Grow?

Did you know that most baby mollusks have no shells? If you saw one of these tiny, transparent creatures swimming around, you'd never guess that it had hard-shelled parents. But living without a shell's protection is dangerous for little mollusks, and most

Snails, like other mollusks, do not have hard shells when they are very young.

begin to develop their shells when they are just a few days old. The shell is formed from the mantle, a sheet of soft flesh that lies between the growing shell and the animal's body. Mineral crystals come from tiny tubes in the mantle. The mineral crystals build up, layer upon layer, to create the hard shell. Some mollusks add on to their shells slowly and continuously. Shells made in this way are very smooth, with no ridges or lines.

Although the insides of oyster shells are smooth, the outsides are ridged.

You can see the growth lines on this Japanese oyster shell.

Other mollusks, such as oysters, pause in between growth periods. The shells of these animals have growth marks, or rings, much like the rings that can be seen on a tree that has been cut down. The more growth rings you count on a shell, the older the mollusk inside the shell is.

Giant Clams, Deadly Cones, and Other Amazing Shelled Animals

Of all the shells in the world, clams are among the most familiar. Maybe you have seen clams at the fish market. Perhaps you've even eaten steamed or stuffed clams at a

Giant clams live in the warm waters of Polynesia.

seafood restaurant. But one clam that will never show up on your dinner plate is the giant clam, which lives on coral reefs in the warm, tropical waters of Polynesia. With a shell that can be more than 4 feet (1.2 meters) wide, this clam is truly a giant, and a dangerous one at that. Like many bivalves, the giant clam rests with its shell partway open. When disturbed, the clam snaps its shell closed. The danger arises because, big as these clams are, they are very hard to see when they are nestled among the brightly colored corals on the reef. If a diver accidentally

When a clam senses danger it quickly closes its shell.

steps into a giant clam, the shell will slam shut with enough force to break a leg. There are many stories of divers being drowned after getting a leg or an arm caught inside the shell of a giant clam.

Giant Gems

As you might guess, giant clams can produce giant pearls.

Like their smaller relatives, giant clams sometimes produce pearls. From these colossal clams come extraordinarily large pearls—sometimes as big as a golf ball. But risking your life to collect one of these giant gems would be a waste of time. Unfortunately for pearl collectors, these huge pearls are not very valuable.

Cones have stingers that can kill worms, fish, and even humans.

Another deadly resident of the tropical seas is the cone, whose poisonous sting can kill a person in a matter of hours. The cone attacks by firing a tiny barbed harpoon that injects a powerful venom into its victim. Cones also get their food this way, using their stingers to paralyze and kill fish, worms, and even other cones.

A scallop can quickly open and close its shell to move through the water.

Another amazing (but completely harmless) mollusk is the common scallop. The scallop is one of the few bivalves that can move around easily. By quickly opening and closing its large, flat shell, the scallop swims through the water in a rapid zigzag pattern. Scallops have even been known to escape from the decks of fishing boats by snapping their shells together, leaping into

The blue dots that line the scallop's shell are actually eyes.

the air, and jumping over-
board. Scallops are also
unusual because they have
many bright blue eyes,
arranged in a long row along
the edges of the shell. Even
with all these eyes, the scallop
doesn't see things very clearly.
A scallop's many eyes just help
it to tell light from dark.

The chambered nautilus,
which has a large coiled shell,
is a close relative of that
famous mollusk without a

shell, the octopus. Like the octopus, the nautilus is a very intelligent animal. It lives deep in the ocean, hunting for food, which it grasps with its many tentacles. Like other shelled creatures, the chambered nautilus adds to its shell during its lifetime. If you were to cut a nautilus shell in half, you would see many small, sealed chambers, and one large chamber at the shell's open end. The small

A nautilus uses its tentacles to grasp food.

You can see the many small chambers of this open nautilus shell.

chambers once provided a home for the nautilus. But as the animal grows bigger, it seals off each old chamber before moving on to larger quarters near the opening of the shell.

Telltale Tentacles

In most mollusks, it is very difficult to tell the male from the female. But the chambered nautilus is an interesting exception. If you ever run into one of these unique animals, you can figure out if it's a boy or a girl by counting its tentacles. Male nautiluses have about 60 tentacles, and females have 94.

Looking at Shells

Collecting and observing shells are great ways to learn more about them, and about the mollusks that once lived inside them. If you live near a beach, take a walk along the waterline to look for shells that have washed up with the tide. On the day after a

Creating a seashell collection is a great way to learn about mollusks (above). The tide brings new seashells onto the beach every day (left).

storm, you may find lots of shells that have been tossed ashore.

These children are examining a mussel shell that they found.

If you don't live near a beach, the best way to create a shell collection is by buying shells. And don't forget about your local seafood restaurant. There you'll find shells from clams, oysters, mussels, and maybe even scallops and snails. Looking at and learning about these "everyday" shells could be your first step on the road to a world-class shell collection!

To Find Out More

Here are some additional resources to help you learn more about seashells:

Books

Abbott, R. Tucker, Herbert Spencer Zim, and Geo Sandstrom. **Seashells of the World.** Golden Books, 1985.

Burton, Jane. **The Nature and Science of Shells.** Gareth Stevens, 1999.

Hansen, Judith. **Seashells in My Pocket: A Child's Nature Guide to Exploring the Atlantic Coast.** Appalachian Mountain Club, 1992.

Robinson, W. Wright. **How Shellmakers Build Their Amazing Homes.** Blackbirch Press, 1999.

⏣ Organizations and Online Sites

Beach Fun
kidexchange.about.com/cs/ seashells

Information about collecting shells, making shell arts and crafts, organizing your shell collection, and beachcombing.

The Conchologists of America
coa.acnatsci.org/conchnet/

Lots of useful information on shells and shell collecting for both adults and kids. The kids section includes fun facts, collecting tips, stories, and poems. A great web site.

Mollusks
cybersleuth-kids.com/ sleuth/Science/Animals/ Mollusks

Find photographs and information on snails and deep-sea mollusks.

Seashells
www.seashells.org

A guide to beachcombing, preserving, and collecting shells. Contains a link to a web site where collectors can buy shells.

Important Words

bivalve a mollusk whose shell is made up of two parts, joined by a hinge

chiton a type of mollusk whose shell is divided into eight plates, somewhat like a coat of armor

gastropod a mollusk whose shell is usually a one-piece spiral, such as a marine or land snail. There are also gastropods without shells, such as slugs.

mantle a sheet of flesh covering the mollusk's body from which the hard shell is formed

mollusk a phylum of animals that have soft bodies protected, in most cases, by hard shells. Snails, mussels, clams, oysters, slugs, and octopuses are all mollusks.

radula a tonguelike organ that snails and some other mollusks use to obtain food

univalve a mollusk whose shell is made of one piece, usually in a spiral shape

Index

Meet the Author

Ann O. Squire has a Ph.D. in animal behavior. Before becoming a writer, she studied African electric fish, rats, and other animals. Dr. Squire has written many books on animals, animal behavior, and other natural science topics. Her most recent books for Children's Press include *Animals of the Sea and Shore, African Animals, Animal Babies*, and *Animal Homes*. She lives with her children, Emma and Evan, in Bedford, New York.

Photographs © 2002: Aaron Norman: 39; Dembinsky Photo Assoc.: 26 (Bill Curtsinger), 1, 17 (E.R. Degginger), cover (Gary Meszaros), 41 left (Fritz Polking); Photo Researchers, NY: 4, 21 (A. Flowers & L. Newman), 28 (David Hall), 41 right (Richard Hutchings), 2 (George D. Lepp), 16 (Fred J. Maroon), 13 (Andrew J. Martinez), 34 (Fred McConnaughey), 24 (Neil B. McDaniel), 9 (Gary Meszaros), 8 (Rita Nannini), 11 (Allan Power), 32 (Dr. Paul A. Zahl); Superstock, Inc.: 38 (Angelo Cavalli), 6; Visuals Unlimited: 42 (Jack Ballard), 29 (Hal Beral), 12 (Gerald & Buff Corsi), 19, 30 (David B. Fleetham), 37 (Alex Kerstitch), 18 (Kjell B. Sandved), 23 (David Sieren), 15 (David Wrobel).